RUBANK EDUCATIONAL LIBRARY No. 78

Selected Studies

Advanced Etudes, Scales and Arpeggios in all Major and Minor Keys

for CLARINET

by H. Voxman

ADVANCED ETUDES

	Page		Page
C Major	2	A Minor	4
F Major	6	D Minor	8
G Major	10	E Minor	12
B♭ Major	14	G Minor	16
D Major	18	B Minor	20
E♭ Major	22	C Minor	24
A Major	26	F# Minor	28
A♭ Major	30	F Minor	32
E Major	34	C# Minor	36
D♭ Major	38	B♭ Minor	40
B Major	42	G# Minor	44
G♭ Major	46	E♭ Minor	48
F# Major	50	D# Minor	52
Cadenza Study			Kreutzer 54

SCALES AND ARPEGGIOS

Scales	56
Scales in Thirds	62
Arpeggios	71

RUBANK®

HAL•LEONARD®
CORPORATION
7777 W. BLUEMOUND RD. P.O. BOX 13819 MILWAUKEE, WI 53213

C Major

FERLING-ROSE

Andante cantabile

Copyright MCMXLII by Rubank, Inc.
International Copyright Secured

Allº agitato

A Minor

HEINZE

Allegretto

F Major

ROMANZE

WIEDEMANN

Andante maestoso

GAMBARO

Allegretto

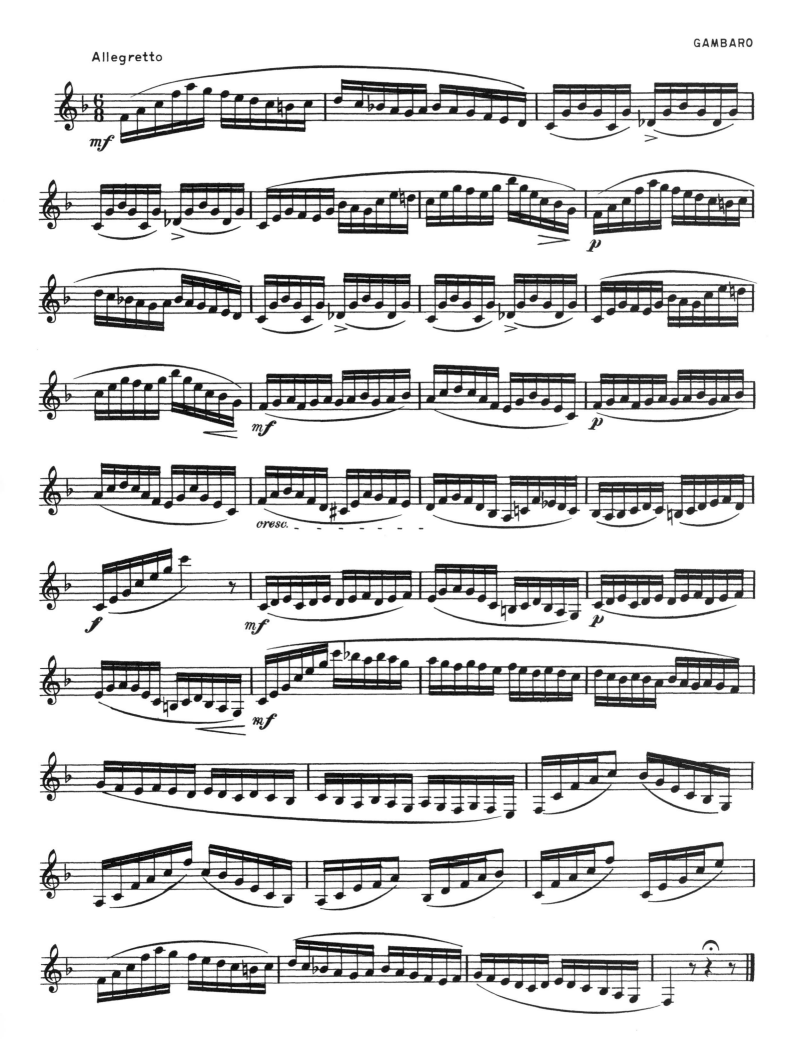

D Minor

FERLING-ROSE

MÜLLER

Allegro moderato

G Major

BOURRÉE

BACH

Allegro vivace

E Minor

HEINZE

B♭ Major

GAMBARO

Adagio cantabile (in 8)

Allegro scherzando (in 3)

G Minor

FERLING - ROSE

HEINZE

D Major

MAZAS

Andante

Allegro assai

B Minor

MÜLLER

Allegro molto

WIEDEMANN

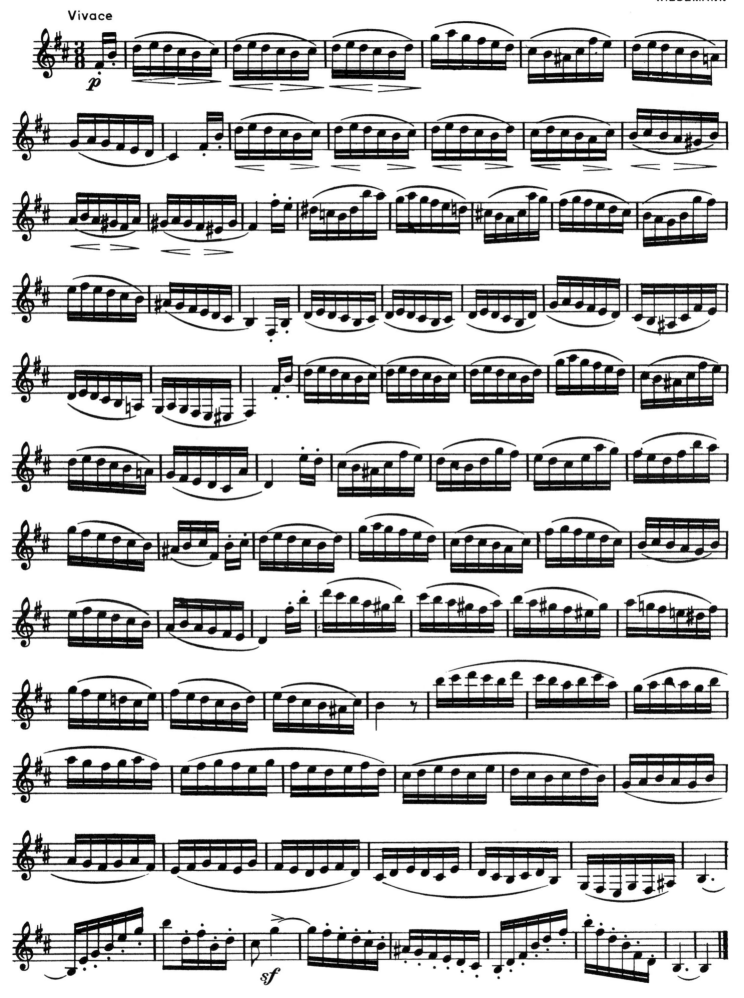

Eb Major

Allegro moderato

C Minor

HEINZE

Allegro

GAMBARO

A Major

FERLING-ROSE

Andante cantabile

MÜLLER

Allegro moderato

F# Minor

BERR

Allegro

A♭ Major

KLOSÉ

Andante

Allegro moderato

F Minor

HEINZE

Allegro con moto

E Major

FERLING-ROSE

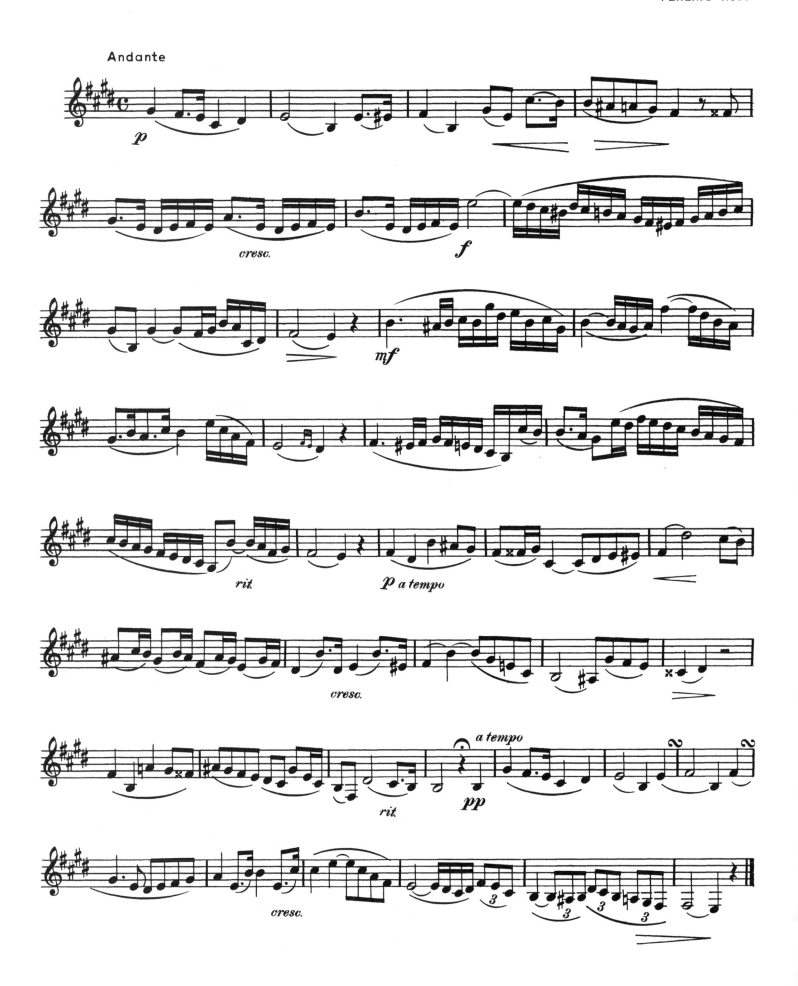

Allegro

C# Minor

HEINZE

D♭ Major

Adagio

MÜLLER

Allegro moderato

B♭ Minor

Allegro molto

mf staccato

B Major

FERLING-ROSE

Andante (in 3)

MÜLLER

G♯ Minor

MÜLLER

Moderato assai (in **4**)

Scherzo

HEINZE

Allegro vivace

Gb Major

MAZAS

Allº moderato, ma brillante

E♭ Minor

HEINZE

Andante cantabile

Allegro

F# Major

MÜLLER

Allegro moderato

D# Minor

HEINZE

BERTINI - BENDER

Allegro

Cadenza Study

KREUTZER

Adagio

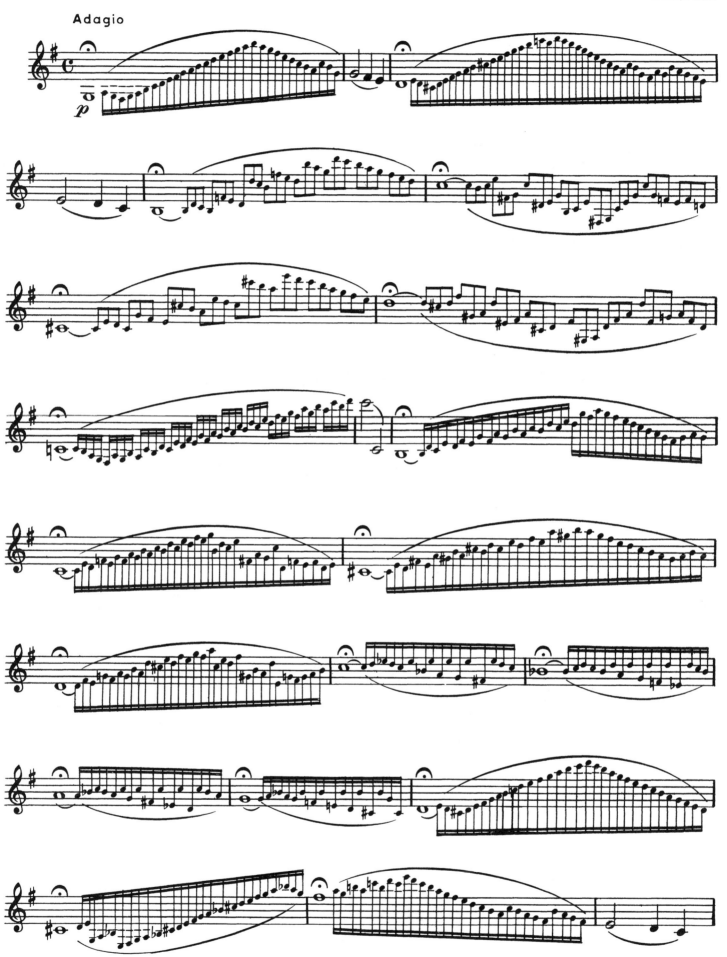

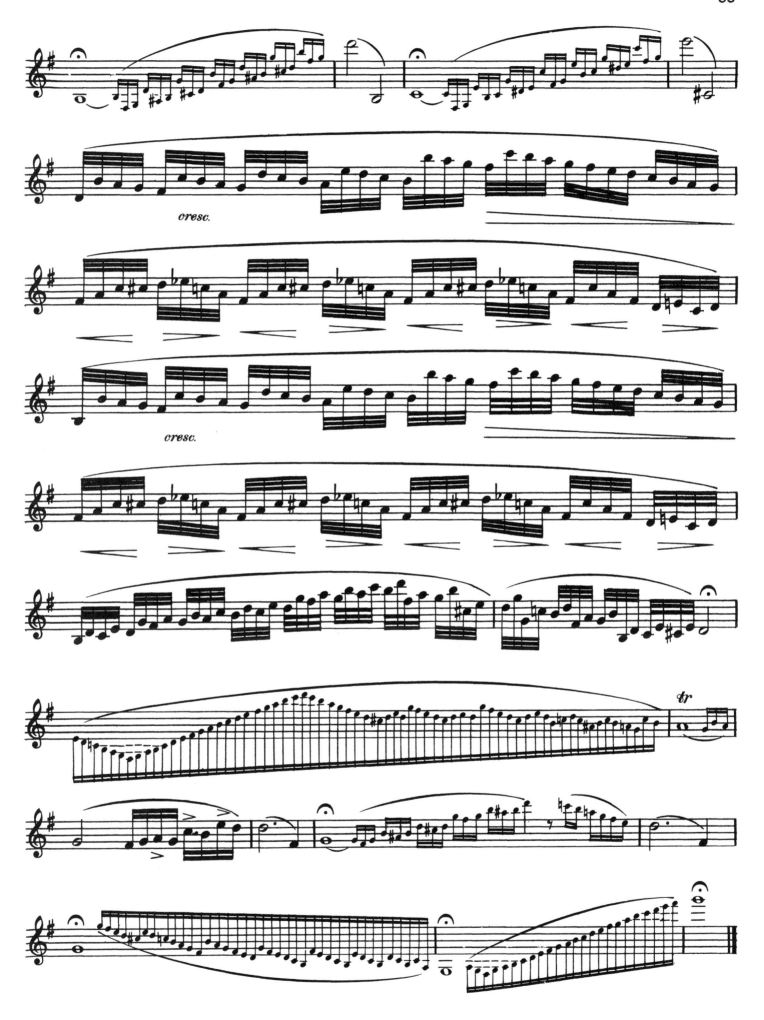

Scales

Adapted from BAERMANN

The use of a metronome with the following studies is highly recommended.

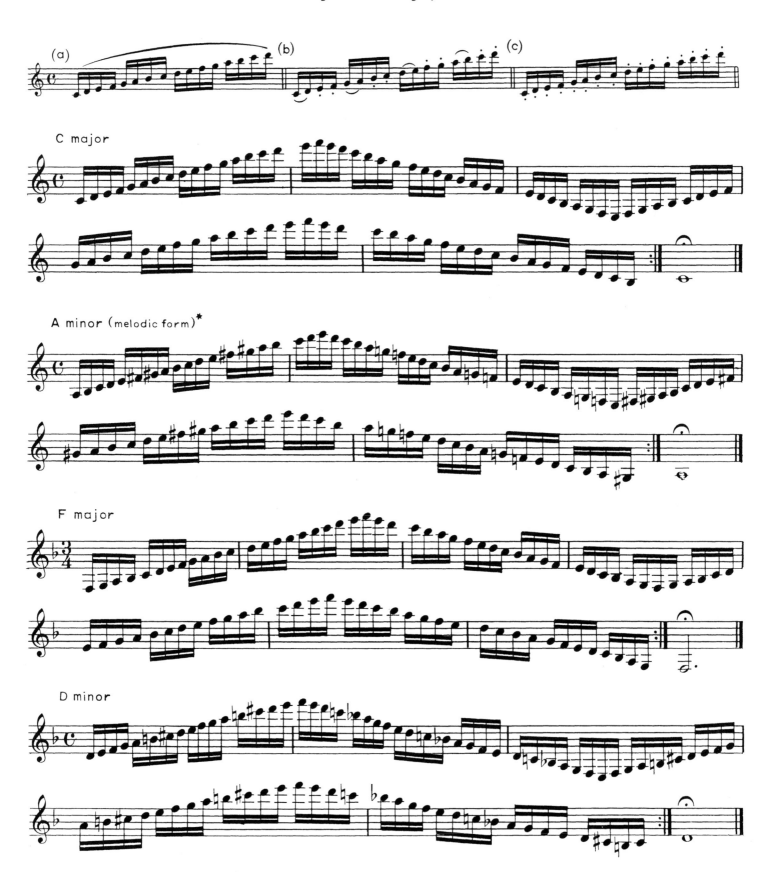

C major

A minor (melodic form)*

F major

D minor

* All minor scale exercises should also be practiced in the harmonic form.

Copyright MCMXLII by Rubank, Inc.
International Copyright Secured

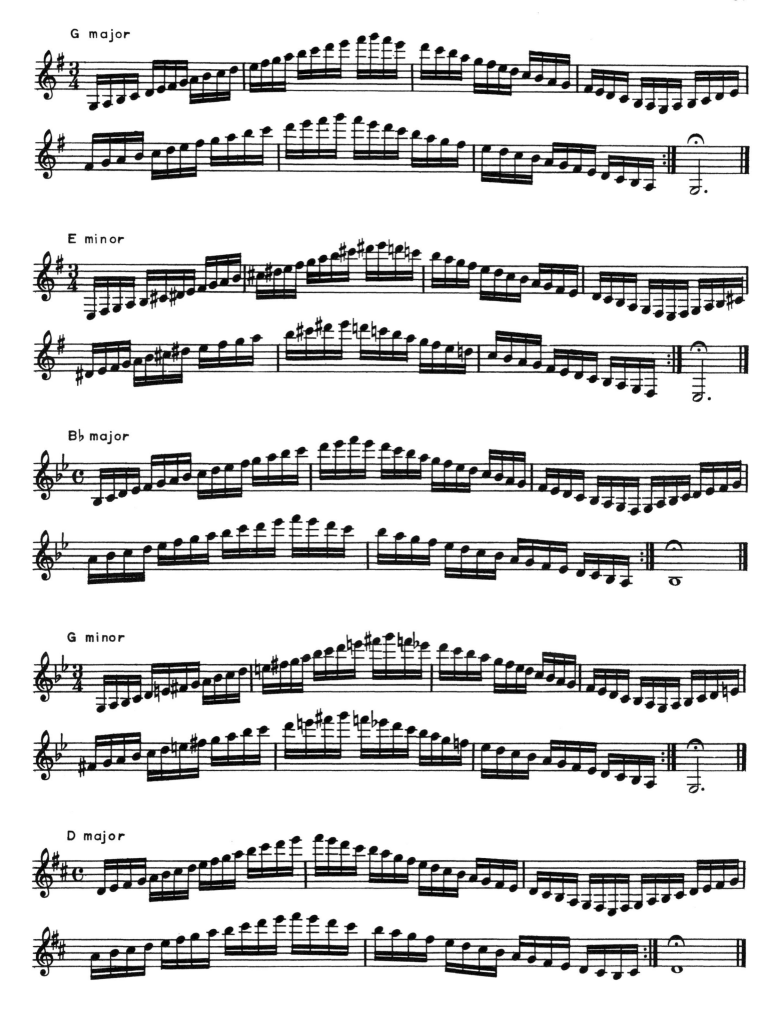

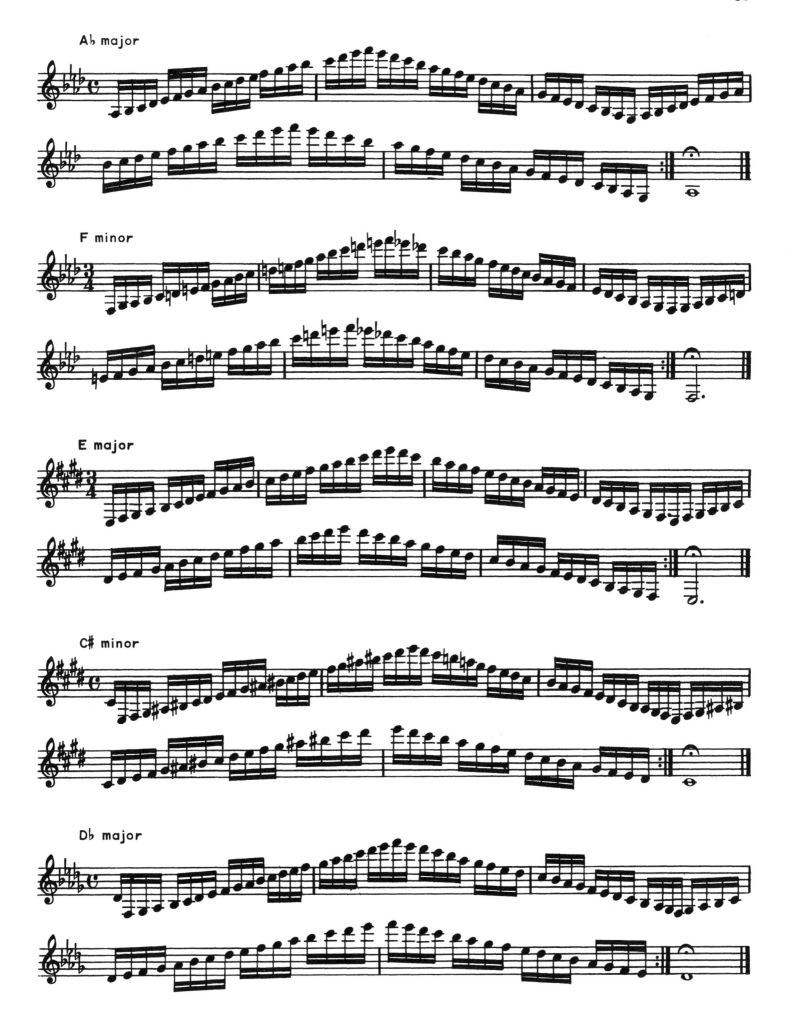

60

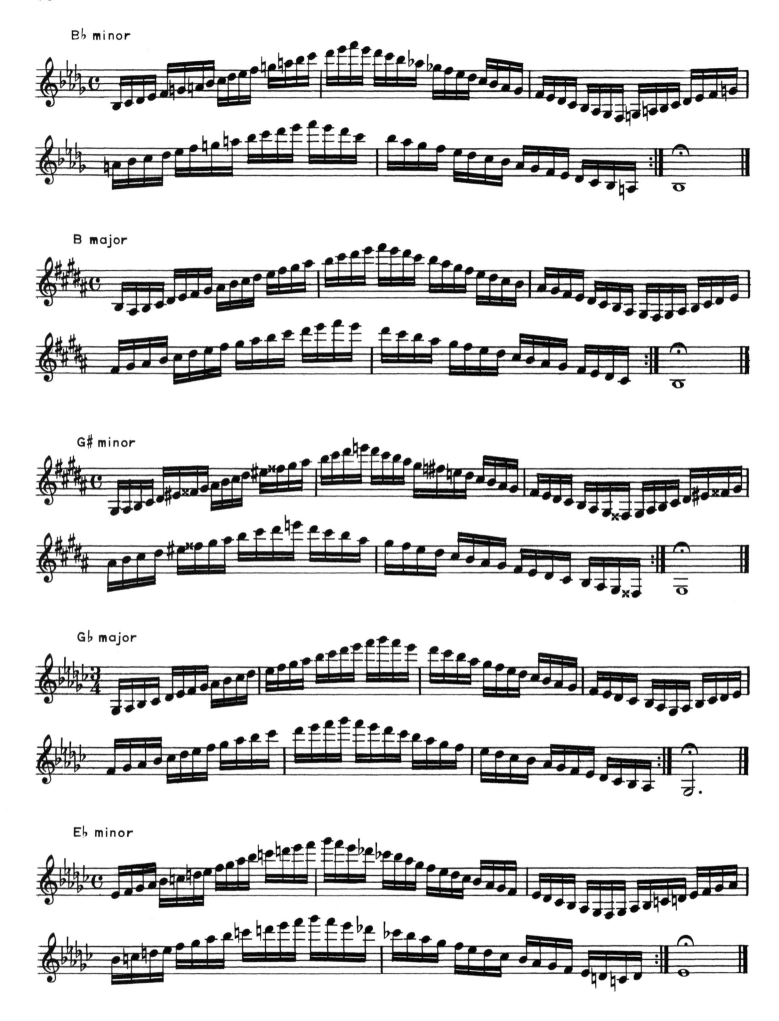

F# major

D# minor

Whole-tone scale on E

Whole-tone scale on F

Chromatic scale

Scales in Thirds

C major

A minor (melodic form)*

F major

* Practice also in the harmonic form.

Copyright MCMXLII by Rubank, Inc.
International Copyright Secured

D minor

G major

E minor

Bb major

G minor

D major

B minor

Eb major

C minor

66

A major

F# minor

Ab major

F minor

E major

C# minor

68

Db major

Bb minor

B major

G# minor

Gb major

Eb minor

Arpeggios

F# major

D# minor

Arpeggio of the augmented 5th

Arpeggio of the augmented 5th